PRAYING
FOR RAIN

BY ROBERT LEWIS VAUGHAN

★

★

DRAMATISTS
PLAY SERVICE
INC.

SPECIAL NOTE

Originally produced by Curious Theatre Company
at the Acoma Center (Chip Walton, Artistic Director)
in Denver, Colorado, March 2000.

For Chris Hubersberger
*   ... for the history*

And for Susie Medak
*   ... for* Long Day's Journey

And my thanks to Paula Vogel
*   ... for Denver*

ACKNOWLEDGMENTS

The Author wishes to thank the following:

Alma Cuervo (my first and always Miss K); Hayley Finn (for stepping up to the plate the first time out); Nicole Graham (all those agent things); Hank Jacobs (hey, buddy); Ilene Jacobs (for baby-sitting William while I was all over the place working on this play); Jocelyn Johnson (for dropping everything to help in Denver); Gary McGettrick (for that magic silver bullet); Eddie Sanchez (for the grand tour and all the guava); The Lady Helen Sneed (for being in my life); Stephen Sultan (for harassing us until we'd let him publish this play — that was cool of him); Paul Tei (for casting high-school kids from the New World School of the Arts in the proper roles and helping to prove to adults that they are, indeed, smart human beings).

PRAYING FOR RAIN was first produced by the Curious Theatre Company (Chip Walton and Britta Erickson, Producers; Kim Mathis, Associate Producer) at The Acoma Center in Denver, Colorado, in March 2000. It was directed by Chip Walton; the set design was by Dave Russell; the lighting design was by William Temple Davis; the original music and sound design were by Matthew E. Morgan; the costume design was by Janice L. Benning; the production stage manager was Victoria N. Buchanan; and the assistant director/dramaturg was Jana Curtis. The cast was as follows:

MISS K	Kathryn Gray
ERIN	Misti McBride
MARC	Gene Gillette
CHRIS	Todd Webster
JIM	Craig Trout
BRIAN	Chris Reid
LIZ	Dee Covington

PRAYING FOR RAIN also received a special presentation by The Gable Stage at the Biltmore in Coral Gables, Florida, in December 2000. It was directed by Joseph Adler. The cast was as follows:

MISS K	Barbara Sloan
ERIN	Claire Murray
MARC	Michael Blum
CHRIS	Max Graham
JIM	David Fink
BRIAN	Laif Gilbertson
LIZ	Monica Pena

CHARACTERS

MARC — 18 or 19

MISS K — 40s

BRIAN — 20s

LIZ — 20s

ERIN — 17

JIM and CHRIS — 19 and 20ish

PLACE

The entire play takes place on The Bluffs at Dragon's Tongue, which is a red sandstone rock formation. Centuries of wind and rain erosion have formed these portions of the Bluffs into what looks like the head of a giant dragon. The downstage side of the head curves up to form the brow and what should look like a horn; the upstage side slopes down to form a snout; a center piece of rock fell decades ago and juts out from the brow and snout and is called the tongue. The dragon seems to be curling its head around, looking off the top of the Bluffs, out over the valley below and toward the mountains a hundred miles away. The Bluffs are studded with pines, framing both sides of the stage, and the sky fills the back of the stage out and past the mountains.

TIME

The past as Marc thinks about it and the present as he sees it.

From too much love of living
From hopes and fears set free
We praise with brief thanksgiving
Whatever gods may be
That no life lives forever
That dead men rise up never
That even the weariest river
Winds somewhere safe to sea.

—Swinburne
The Garden of Persephone

PRAYING FOR RAIN

ACT ONE

House to half: Music begins to play — softly — we don't want to frighten the audience yet. When the song kicks in, the house lights go out and the volume goes up. Total darkness.

At rise: The song is still playing in the dark. A moment and a few stars appear in the black sky. The music stops. Light illuminates only Marc's face. We hear Miss K's voice whisper, "What is your history?" Stars start filling the sky and we see Marc standing alone at Dragon's Tongue. Brian walks out onto the rock. He stares down at Marc and takes a photograph. A moment and the stars fade to black.

As the lights come back up, the men are gone and Miss K is sitting alone grading papers. Erin stomps in and stops, glaring at her mother. Long pause.

MISS K. … yeeeeessss…?
ERIN. You know.
MISS K. Do I?
ERIN. Do you have any idea how embarrassing this is?
MISS K. I must not.
ERIN. I'm not kidding. Mother.
MISS K. Erin?

ERIN. What?

MISS K. What's your problem?

ERIN. All my friends are pissed off at me and Annie Weaver won't even talk to me now.

MISS K. What did you do?

ERIN. I didn't do anything! You did! You're always doing things like this to me and I want it to stop. So...?

MISS K. What did I do this time?

ERIN. You're working with Marc.

MISS K. Yes, I am. *(Pause.)*

ERIN. Well ... don't.

MISS K. What?

ERIN. Don't. Make somebody else do it.

MISS K. That's not possible.

ERIN. Why not?

MISS K. Because I'm a teacher and it's —

ERIN. Well, there are other teachers and since I'm your daughter and I go there I think you should take me into consideration just once and make somebody else work with him so I can walk down the hall and not have to — so just do it, Mom.

MISS K. It's too late. They'll get over it.

ERIN. I won't.

MISS K. Yes, you will.

ERIN. I'm not kidding. I don't want you working with him.

MISS K. That's just too bad. Now you listen to me —

ERIN. This is my problem too, now, and it isn't fair to me that ...

MISS K. They'll get over it. You'll get over it. Everybody will get over it.

ERIN. Not this time. Not with Marc, Mother.

MISS K. I've never in my life seen a bunch of kids turn on somebody as fast as you and everybody else in that school turned on Marc McGettrick, and I barely even know him.

ERIN. He turned on himself first, Mother, and — what do you mean you barely know him? How can you not know him?

MISS K. I know of him — what he used to be ... but somehow, I never had him in one of my classes, so that's why I'm doing the sessions with him.

ERIN. Please ... just ask somebody else to —

10

MISS K. It's the history, Erin, that he needs. I'm the only one there is ...

ERIN. So I'm just ...

MISS K. I'm doing my job. You keep this up and I'll volunteer to chaperone your senior prom, young lady. *(Erin starts out but stops. With her back to her mother:)*

ERIN. Tomorrow when I get to school ... I'm joining the Young Republicans ... *(She walks out and the lights fade. In the darkness we hear the beat of the song for a moment, then the lights come up in the classroom. Marc enters.)*

MARC. So ... I'm here. I'm not late or nothin' ...

MISS K. You can sit down. Marc McGettrick.

MARC. Yeah.

MISS K. Why are you here, Marc?

MARC. Mr. Lange said I wouldn't get to come back to school or graduate unless I —

MISS K. I know that part. By heart. Why ... are you here?

MARC. ... I f — messed up. I ... this is all gonna be history?

MISS K. For four weeks.

MARC. They didn't tell me to bring any books or nothing.

MISS K. Why are you here?

MARC. I got busted tryin' to make a deal to sell a gun, okay?

MISS K. On school grounds?

MARC. It was stupid and I —

MISS K. — shouldn't have done it and ... I know. I know. Who'd you try to sell it to?

MARC. What?

MISS K. Who'd you try to sell the gun to?

MARC. Some kid. I don't even ... I didn't have the gun, okay? I didn't have the gun on me.

MISS K. I know that — you wouldn't be here if you had. You should have tried to make the deal with Patrick Sisson. He'd have forked over the money real fast and you probably wouldn't have gotten caught. Quick exchange, no haggling.

MARC. This ... so ... Uh —

MISS K. Isn't that what happened?

MARC. I guess ... yeah.

MISS K. Patrick saw me at the Quick Stop once. I'd locked my keys

11

in the car and before I knew it, he had the car door open, was sitting behind the wheel, had the engine running and told me I needed a tune-up. I like Patrick. He must have a lot of interesting tools hidden in that big coat he always wears. Do you know each other?

MARC. No, not really.

MISS K. I can see Patrick buying or selling ... a ... your records don't indicate that you would have done this and you don't strike me as ...

MARC. I never did anything like that before. It's not like I'm some sort of ... I don't know ...

MISS K. You had Mr. Abernathy for history.

MARC. Yeah.

MISS K. You didn't do very well.

MARC. No.

MISS K. Why?

MARC. I don't know. You know? I mean ...

MISS K. It's okay, you can tell me.

MARC. He's just ... I don't know ... It's like —

MISS K. Is it because he spits when he talks or because he has dandruff?

MARC. ... what...?

MISS K. Where were you going to get the gun?

MARC. What the fuck...? What ... I mean...? I'm sorry I ...

MISS K. I can't believe you just said that!

MARC. I'm sorry — I'm just, I just ...

MISS K. I'm kidding you.

MARC. Can we do history now?

MISS K. No. I thought we should spend this first hour together ... just getting to know a little about each other.

MARC. This is ...

MISS K. ... what...?

MARC. I mean I really want to do this history stuff and I really want them to let me come back to school so I can graduate.

MISS K. Tell me where you were going to get the gun.

MARC. Is this some weird trick counseling shit? They know, okay? I already — it's not like I pulled out an automatic and blew half the kids in the cafeteria away.

MISS K. I know that, Marc —

MARC. Then this isn't fair, because they told me if I did the suspension and did this make-up detention thing that —

MISS K. No counseling. This is just a make-up-detention-history-thing. The board'll only know about whether or not you make the grade you need and that your behavior is acceptable. Otherwise our conversations are between us.

MARC. It's because he spits, has dandruff and gets all in your face when he asks you questions.

MISS K. You know he's my husband. *(Silence.)*

MARC. ... you're goofin' ... right?

MISS K. Yes.

MARC. You're ... like ...

MISS K. Four weeks. *(Pause.)* Are you frightened? I didn't mean to frighten you.

MARC. No. I mean ... no.

MISS K. You look uncomfortable.

MARC. Can we do history?

MISS K. It doesn't say anywhere in your file that you were this eager to learn. There must be a mistake ...

MARC. Do you know Jim Borrowman and Chris Brown?

MISS K. Chris Brown graduated last year. Jim...?

MARC. Yeah.

MISS K. Why?

MARC. Jim and Chris had a gun. They made me try to sell it. — Asked me to ...

MISS K. I don't remember Jim Bor —

MARC. He dropped out a while ago.

MISS K. How do you know them?

MARC. Chris lives across the street from me.

MISS K. So this sale was just a neighborly thing to do?

MARC. Why do you wanna know?

MISS K. I don't know.

MARC. Why are you messin' with me like this?

MISS K. I told you I just think we should get to know one another a little. Do you know a better way than spending this first session talking —

MARC. Yeah, but —

MISS K. I could just have you open a textbook and pretend I

don't know why you're here. We could just sit here not saying anything to each other and stretch the four weeks into what feels like four months … would you prefer that?

MARC. Well …

MISS K. Well…?

MARC. Were you afraid of me?

MISS K. Afraid of you? Why would I —

MARC. When they wouldn't let me back in school and I … I saw Miss Jameson one day and she looked at me like … she started actin' all like she was … I don't know … like I was gonna …

MISS K. What you did makes people more than a little nervous, Marc. That's why they chose me to work with you. I never had you in one of my classes and shouldn't have a preconceived … well … shouldn't …

MARC. So you got stuck with me?

MISS K. No. I didn't have to do this. We aren't required to stay after school and tutor students or supervise detentions. I volunteered to do this. I could be at home going through the *Globe* and the *Star* figuring out which articles to read to my ninety-three-year-old Granny this Saturday morning, but I decided to do this instead.

MARC. How come you like that Patrick guy?

MISS K. Because I used to live next door to the Sissons before I moved to Aspen Street and I've known him since he was a little baby. He was in some of my classes when I was teaching in junior high. And … if I keep being nice to him … he'll fix my car.

MARC. Do you like … are you …

MISS K. You really messed up, didn't you? *(Silence.)*

MARC. We should do history or …

MISS K. We don't have to do history the way you think of it. And you can cool your jets. You only have two tests to redo and we have plenty of time for that.

MARC. Fou weeks.

MISS K. Why do you think Mr. Lange went out of his way to help you?

MARC. Help me?

MISS K. He personally asked the board not to expel you. That isn't Mr. Lange the Principal at all. That was Mr. Lange the man we all rarely see and I think you know that.

MARC. I don't know. I guess … he knew I never got in trouble, really, before …

MISS K. You'll be eighteen when you graduate?

MARC. I'm already … yeah. I am.

MISS K. You know you could have gone to jail? What do you want to be when you grow up?

MARC. You are too weird, man.

MISS K. That's what my daughter always tells me.

MARC. … you're Erin's mom …

MISS K. Do you know her?

MARC. I kind of did. We used to talk and … Not really.

MISS K. For a minute I was —

MARC. What, worried that she was hanging out with some kid like me who's tryin' to sell shit to kids —

MISS K. Whoa — I was thinking, "Great, another friend she doesn't want me to meet because she doesn't want me to embarrass her," for your information. Maybe we should do —

MARC. I'm sorry.

MISS K. Why'd you stop playing sports?

MARC. Why would you embarrass Erin? *(Pause.)*

MISS K. Because it's fun. I don't really, but she thinks I do. It all started when we were shopping once. She hates shopping with me now, but — I … I love clowns. I collect clowns and, we were leaving the mall, and I saw a clown on a shelf in a shop and I just lost it. The store was closing but I had to have that clown, and I was rattling the gates begging them to let me in so I could buy that clown. Erin thought I'd lost my mind and some of her friends were walking by and they saw us and Erin … You answer me. Why'd you quit playing sports?

MARC. I messed up my back and my knees on my brother's bike. I was in the hospital for a while. They said I could never … You don't seem like Erin's mom.

MISS K. I tried, but she's rebelling and is turning out to be very conservative.

MARC. She's great at track.

MISS K. How long were you in the hospital?

MARC. Like for a month.

MISS K. You wanted to play — your files say you were —

MARC. It would have been fun ... I guess. I mean ... whatever, now ... right?

MISS K. You stopped doing well in your classes after your accident.

MARC. Yeah ...

MISS K. So what do you want to do?

MARC. What does Erin want to do?

MISS K. She won't tell me. But I do know that she's thinking of broadcasting.

MARC. What do you mean she won't tell you?

MISS K. I'm her mother and I also teach here. She doesn't think she can ever escape me so she pretends I don't exist and does her best to ignore me and keep things from me. Patrick Sisson said to her — "You should be nice to your mom, man." I love him —

MARC. Do you like, hang out with Pat?

MISS K. No, of course not, but he comes over now and then.

MARC. To see Erin?

MISS K. Yes ... and to see me. To say hi. To see if I need anything done.

MARC. What does Mr. K think?

MISS K. Who?

MARC. Mr. Kra — your husband?

MISS K. ... divorced.

MARC. My mom is too. Well. From my dad. I mean, I guess. Like, I have my dad's last name, but he's my mom's ... I don't have my real dad's last name but I have my mom's second ...

MISS K. Okay. (Silence.)

MARC. Can we do history now please?

MISS K. Marc ... I want you to know that when you're here with me for the next four weeks you can be yourself. I want you to —

MARC. Alright ...

MISS K. I mean it. If we're discussing something, I want to hear what you have to say, I don't want you to tell me what you think I want to hear.

MARC. Well isn't what you want to hear right?

MISS K. No. We won't be doing flash cards with dates. Our history will be open to discussion.

MARC. Yeah, but I need ...

MISS K. What's your history? (The lights darken on them. In the

16

mountains and at Dragon's Tongue the sun sets: blood red. Miss K and the desks are gone, leaving Marc alone as the sunset engulfs him. The song blasts. Brian appears on Dragon's Tongue and photographs Marc. After the flash, the stage is dark and the music is gone. In the darkness, Marc lights a cigarette. As the lights come up he is leaning against a wall. He's watching someone off.)

MARC. Hey. HEY! *(Pause.)* Hey Erin! *(A moment and Erin, dressed in running clothes, trots onstage.)*

ERIN. What?

MARC. I just, you know, wanted to say you looked good out there.

ERIN. Thanks. *(She starts off.)*

MARC. That's it? Why won't you talk to me anymore?

ERIN. Sorry. I'm kinda ... How's your back?

MARC. It's fine. My knees are still all fucked up but ... you know.

ERIN. Are you gonna be able to play again?

MARC. Probably not. It's okay though.

ERIN. Why do you say that? You were —

MARC. It's no big deal. I mean, it's not like —

ERIN. Whatever, I gotta — *(She starts off again.)*

MARC. So, like, since I don't play anymore you can't talk to me?

ERIN. ... No ...

MARC. Yeah, right.

ERIN. Where's Chris and Jim?

MARC. Why?

ERIN. It's too early to be out rolling drunks on McMasters and lately I haven't seen you without them lurking somewhere nearby. So ...

MARC. They're alright.

ERIN. They're criminals.

MARC. No they aren't.

ERIN. Bull shit, Marc.

MARC. They don't roll drunks either.

ERIN. Janet Vasquez told me they got busted a month ago for trying to roll some drunk guy outside the Baby Doll.

MARC. Once.

ERIN. Yeah, right.

MARC. So ... I wasn't there, I didn't do anything.

ERIN. Yet.

MARC. What's that supposed to mean?

ERIN. You hang out with them too much. Ever since you got in that accident, you ... It's like you don't care about anything. You don't ...

MARC. What else is there to do around this place? It's not like I can —

ERIN. Whatever, Marc. I gotta —

MARC. Wait. Don't go yet.

ERIN. What?

MARC. Nothing. I just ... *(He lights another cigarette using his first.)*

ERIN. I'm really sorry Marc.

MARC. Really? Why?

ERIN. That's another thing. It's like you dare people to not like you anymore. You're like, acting like you're all that, and you never did that before. Were you just waiting for me so you could —

MARC. I wasn't doing anything. I like watching you run. I really —

ERIN. Yeah?

MARC. No.

ERIN. You make me sad.

MARC. Why's that?

ERIN. You died after you — I mean ... You almost died ...

MARC. Well, I didn't really —

ERIN. Almost.

MARC. I guess.

ERIN. Were you scared?

MARC. Yeah, I guess. When I knew. I didn't know until I wasn't gonna die that I almost died. So. It was kinda like ... well I'm not but I almost did ... so.

ERIN. Nobody in my family's even dead yet. Well, my great-grampa died before I was born, but great-gramma's like really old. My mom says she's not gonna die until my uncle gets to be Pope. He's a monsignor at the Vatican.

MARC. Really?

ERIN. Yeah. He's nice.

MARC. I don't have any famous relatives. I don't even feel like I have relatives.

ERIN. He isn't famous. What do you mean?

MARC. Nobody in my family even talks really and I don't remember any of our other relatives.

ERIN. Your dad's your step dad, right?

MARC. Yeah. My real dad's ... he never comes around.

ERIN. Where is he now?

MARC. I think he's in California or someplace like that.

ERIN. Do you miss him?

MARC. I don't really know him, and ... you know ... my step dad, so ...

ERIN. He and your mom still fight?

MARC. Sometimes. I just leave. You know. Whatever.

ERIN. People don't really make fun of your mom, you know. I know you're all embarrassed and stuff, and think people laugh at you, but they don't. You should just —

MARC. — Whatever ... you don't really know what it's —

ERIN. Well ... I should ... *(She starts out again.)*

MARC. Erin, wait. Please? I'm ... *(She stops.)* Do you wanna maybe ... hang out ... sometime ... or something...?

ERIN. ... well ... I'm. I'm kinda going out with ...

MARC. ... yeah ...

ERIN. I think your boys are coming this way ... *(She looks off; he turns.)*

MARC. ... I mean, just to hang out. Not like anything ... you know ...

ERIN. Yeah. Sure ... *(She starts off.)* See ya, Marc. *(She's gone. He looks off. He'd hide if he could. The "boys" enter.)*

CHRIS. What's up, bitch?

MARC. Nothin'.

JIM. Where'd she go?

MARC. I don't know. She went to change or something.

CHRIS. Stuck-up bitch ain't said two words to me since I known her.

JIM. Check this out, kid ... *(He pulls a gun which he has tucked into his pants.)*

MARC. What're you gonna do with that?

JIM. Fuckin'. Fuck does it matter? Sell it maybe? This is the shit, kid. *(Jim waves the gun in Marc's face.)*

MARC. Get that thing the fuck outta my face, Jim, man — shit ...

JIM. It ain't loaded —

CHRIS. — yet ...

19

MARC. Whatever.

CHRIS. Give me a smoke.

JIM. What's up with you? Erin get you all —

CHRIS. — all that bitch thinks about is runnin'. She's a dyke, too.

MARC. She is not and don't call her bitch.

JIM. Sports-boy's still lookin' uptown —

CHRIS. Give me a smoke —

JIM. (Pushing Chris away.) Get your fuckin' ass over to the Quick Stop and get some. I'll meet you over there later.

CHRIS. Damn ... man. (Chris goes.)

MARC. I gotta — (He starts off.)

JIM. You goin' to the Bluffs tonight?

MARC. Naw ... I gotta ... (Jim grabs Marc's arm as he starts to walk off.)

JIM. You're shittin' yourself if you think any of those guys are still gonna like you. They only liked you 'cause you could play better than them anyway. Well, guess what? You can't play anymore and they'll start stayin' away from you like you stink. Erin didn't even want to get caught talkin' to you just now so if you think you're gonna get some of her, you're ...

MARC. Shut the fuck up, Jim — you're full of —

JIM. Your mom don't help either so —

MARC. She ... my mom —

JIM. I never say anything about your mom. She don't bother me. I'm just sayin' ... You're the one that always didn't want anybody to know she's your mom if you could help it. You know what I mean? I'm just sayin'...? Just remember who your friends are, kid ... Those fuckin' kids walked away from you. We didn't ...

MARC. Nobody ... walked away from me ... I'm ...

JIM. Whatever, kid. You'll be at the Bluffs tonight, just like you were there last time we went. You know who your friends are ... (Jim backs away, watching Marc as he leaves. The lights slowly fade as Marc moves back to the classroom and sits at his desk. He tries to page through a book. Miss K enters.)

MISS K. Why are you here so early? Did you miss me?

MARC. No. I just. Well.

MISS K. I've heard you speak in complete sentences.

MARC. Like, how old are you?

MISS K. Like, none of your business.

MARC. How long have you been a teacher here?

MISS K. This isn't about my history, Marc. It's about yours.

MARC. You used to teach at the junior high.

MISS K. Yes, I did.

MARC. You must have been really young?

MISS K. It was my first teaching job. I was there until about five years ago when Mr. Lange and Ms. Cisneros and I got smarter so they let us come to high school. *(Pause.)*

MARC. Do you like high school better?

MISS K. Do you?

MARC. Yeah. I hated junior high.

MISS K. Why?

MARC. Because. It was like ... nothing ... I — played sports but ... I just — it was like nobody really liked anybody else and even if you knew kids before it was like you didn't know 'em anymore and ... except for Jim and Chris ... and I don't know, it was just like sleepwalkin' in a bad dream for three years ... you know?

MISS K. No. Why are you asking me these questions? *(Jim and Chris slink up onto Dragon's Tongue. In the murky lighting they look like animals stalking prey. They stare at Marc. Pause.)*

MARC. ... because ... my mom said I had to treat you right.

MISS K. Thank her for me, but I'm not worried about you.

MARC. No. She said you were cool, and that you were the only one that treated her right, and that I wasn't supposed to fu — mess with you ...

MISS K. I treated her right? ... What do ...

MARC. You taught my mom, Miss K.

MISS K. ... really...?

MARC. ... yeah ...

MISS K. I did...?

MARC. ... yeah ...

MISS K. ... oh my god ...

MARC. ... yeah ...

MISS K. ... Really...?

MARC. ... I know ...

MISS K. Oh my god ...

MARC. You didn't know that?

MISS K. I don't think I made the connection …

MARC. Well, like you're a teacher.

MISS K. I've been teaching for nearly twenty-five years, Marc.

MARC. Don't you —

MISS K. I remember some, a lot of my students, but I've had a lot of students. Your mom…?

MARC. Celia McGettrick.

MISS K. Who was she then?

MARC. Oh. Celia Lujan. *(Silence.)* Do you know her? *(Pause.)*

MISS K. I think I remember her.

MARC. Yeah?

MISS K. Your father … is … Danny Turner.

MARC. You knew him too?

MISS K. They were some of my first students.

MARC. Wow … huh?

MISS K. Yeah.

MARC. My mom says I have to be cool with you.

MISS K. Yeah. *(Brian and Liz enter and begin setting up a picnic. Jim keeps his eyes trained on Marc as Chris focuses on Brian and Liz.)*

MARC. I guess this is a little weird for me.

MISS K. For you?

MARC. Well, yeah. I mean you …

MISS K. I'm fully aware that many of my students have grown up and become adults and have lives and … I just … I am always amazed that …

MARC. Yeah, well, I know my mom was a kid once too and that she went to school and everything but I didn't think I'd have to know her teachers too.

MISS K. I was very young to be teaching.

MARC. Yeah, well, I guess.

MISS K. Your dad was …

MARC. I don't really remember him.

MISS K. I'm sorry.

MARC. No big deal.

MISS K. I think I remember I liked your dad.

MARC. You like guys who get in trouble.

MISS K. He didn't get in trouble until after I knew him.

MARC. I guess. *(The picnic is set up. Brian is putting his camera together.)*

MISS K. Listen to me, Marc. You … you are not in trouble anymore. This is your chance to … you know I coach Matters of the Mind, right?

MARC. Yeah. No, but, yeah, I've heard of it.

MISS K. I'm one of the Problem Captains when we go to competitions. My problem is the Spontaneous Question. The students don't know in advance what the problem is. They enter a room with the judges and then get the question. They have to solve the problem on the spot — no advance time. Right then and there.

MARC. So?

MISS K. Think about it.

MARC. I never did any of that Mind stuff.

MISS K. This is your problem: You got into some trouble that could have ruined your life but you were given a second chance. What are you going to do with that chance?

MARC. What do you mean? *(Brian takes a photograph of Liz. Miss K walks out. He stands and starts after her. The desk and chairs are gone.)* Wait — but … *(Jim crawls off Dragon's Tongue and circles Brian and Liz. Chris moves to the edge of the rock and looks down on them. Marc turns up toward the couple as Brian takes another photograph.)* This isn't fair.

JIM. *(An odd, distorted, animal whisper.)* What's your history, Marco, huh?

MARC. I gotta … I have to … I can't … *(He runs off. Chris stretches out on the rock and Jim sits against a tree as they watch the couple. Jim lights a cigarette; Chris gives a loud yawn.)*

LIZ. I was thinking —

BRIAN. I love the way you do that —

LIZ. Shut up and listen to me. I think we should call your mom and have her come out when my mom comes.

BRIAN. I guess we could … I guess they —

LIZ. They haven't seen each other since the wedding. I don't know when they would, either, unless it was a holiday and … They got along so well. I think it would be fun.

BRIAN. That would be. Uh.

LIZ. It's just an idea, Brian.

BRIAN. I know. I know.

LIZ. We don't have to decide right now.

BRIAN. Yeah. I know. *(He looks at her. Knows she has something else up her sleeve.)*

LIZ. What?

BRIAN. Is there? Are you? What're you...?

LIZ. Nothing.

BRIAN. Liz.

LIZ. Brian.

BRIAN. Why're you looking at me that way?

LIZ. Your hair's messy.

BRIAN. It is not. *(She starts to mess with his hair.)* Okay, stop it. We'll call her. We'll call ...

LIZ. We have plenty of time ... *(The wind begins to blow and the lights slowly fade. Liz leaves, then everyone leaves Brian alone on the bluff. It is sunset. Stunning colors fill the sky over the valley and the mountains in the distance. Brian takes many pictures of Dragon's Tongue. A few moments and Marc walks out onto the rock. Brian looks at Marc.)*

MARC. I was kinda hoping ...

BRIAN. Hoping what?

MARC. That you could help me.

BRIAN. How could I help you? I can't ... help you.

MARC. Just — just — *(He starts down off the rock. Brian steps back.)* — please...?

BRIAN. I don't think so.

MARC. Just talk to me.

BRIAN. About what?

MARC. Just —

BRIAN. What do we have to say to each other?

MARC. I don't know how to ... to ...

BRIAN. I want you to leave me alone.

MARC. Did you ever play sports, or, I mean, did you always just want to do the camera thing?

BRIAN. ... the camera thing ... the Camera Thing ...

MARC. You know, doing photography?

BRIAN. Taking photographs. Being a photographer.

MARC. Yeah.

BRIAN. I always wanted to be a photographer.

24

MARC. How do you know?

BRIAN. I know. I just ... I knew.

MARC. Did you like ... I mean ... how...?

BRIAN. What do you want?

MARC. Did you ... was it because ... *(Silence.)* Did you ... do you ... did it? Did — because ... you loved it?

BRIAN. I knew —

MARC. — you loved it. Because it was what you loved? Did you ever play sports?

BRIAN. A little, for fun. Not much. I loved basketball, but I wasn't very good at it.

MARC. I loved playing sports. God I ... I was great at football and baseball and I really loved that. I didn't care too much about anything else. My grades were always okay and like, I passed, and didn't have to worry about getting kicked off the teams, so ... God I ... And there was this girl, Erin...? She did track. And. Well. I mean, I was ... I wasn't like one of the rich kids, and didn't ... Erin wasn't either but she was really popular, and we kind of hung around with different people, but she was always nice though ... I kind of liked her. A lot. I mean I ... It was like ... what was my history?

BRIAN. What?

MARC. Like ... what was my history? I didn't think about that? You know? I was ... I was gonna be eighteen soon and ... I'm just some kid, you know? I'm just some dumb kid that thought everything was kind of okay. You know? I was really good at what I loved doing when I was a sophomore and then when I was a junior ... And nobody in my family ever even like thought about college, you know? They never mentioned anything like that — it was like — when are you gonna get a job. But at school they were talking to me about college. My stupid brother dropped out of school and just works where he can ... I mean. I don't know what he ever cared about. But they were talking to me about ... How do you know what people care about? How do you know what you care about?

BRIAN. You care when you feel something ... inside ... you care when —

MARC. It's like you just know. Right? I had girlfriends ... A lot ... but — I mostly thought about Erin, though. I tried to really talk to her sometimes. She made me feel ... I ... she just made me feel — and she didn't make me feel stupid ... for talking to her. It just seemed like — then — that time, for me, was like — all it was ever gonna be, like — it would be good. Then I ... *(Silence. Marc lights a cigarette.)* I fucked up on my brother's bike. He had this junked-up Harley that he got for really cheap from this guy he worked with? And. I don't really know what happened. I guess. I mean, I remember a few things like ... I don't know. My back was all messed up and my knees. And there was some piece of metal in my stomach. Check this — *(Marc lifts his shirt to show off his scar as he moves toward Brian. What we really notice is a gun tucked into his jeans.)* I mean it kind of goes up and around my side, like, but this wasn't anything compared to —

BRIAN. What about the gun?

MARC. What's my history?

BRIAN. Is that your —

MARC. Maybe the accident. No. This. Yeah. *(Marc pulls out the gun.)*

BRIAN. Why?

MARC. After ... it was the only time ... Erin was the only one who ... After I came back from being suspended, she came up to me and, I don't know, it looked like she wanted to cry or was so pissed off at me that she, well ... *(Erin storms on toward Marc.)*

ERIN. I heard what you did. I can't believe you, Marc. I can't believe you! How could you be that stupid? I mean ... Did you get some kind of brain damage in that accident too? Huh?

MARC. No. I —

ERIN. For god's sake, Marc!? Did you at least take the bullets out?

MARC. There weren't any yet. Chris was gonna get 'em. I didn't want ...

ERIN. Why did you do it? *(Silence.)* Why, Marc?

MARC. Because ... I ... I wanted some of the money, okay?

ERIN. You're full of shit. You know that?

MARC. Look, some kid wants a gun, okay? He put the word out. It's not like I was pushin' something on him, okay? So just remember that — he was lookin' and Jim and Chris had what he was lookin' for and they asked me to ...

ERIN. You always seemed so ... You ... we ... It's hard to be your friend, Marc. It was hard to be your friend because ... for whatever reason, you never let anybody get too near you ... But I never thought you'd do something like this. I always thought you'd be able to ... I never thought you were that stupid. Even thinking about selling a gun to a thirteen-year-old is stupid. Every step you've taken in the last two years has been in the wrong stupid direction. You know it?

MARC. I know. I know —

ERIN. Did you even wonder what he wanted that gun for? Huh? When a thirteen-year-old wants a gun ... and worse that he was willing to give you the money and then follow you to some ... wherever ... to get it ... sick ... you're all —

MARC. Did you know that was the first time I ever thought you cared about me? And then it was too late. *(Pause. To Brian:)* After that what was I gonna be doing? Huh? I mess myself up over summer and then I have to go be a senior and I can't be who I used to be because I couldn't play any sports anymore. And then ... that ...

BRIAN. So ... what? You turn eighteen and your life is over?

MARC. I thought that.

BRIAN. What bullshit.

ERIN. I agree.

MARC. How was I supposed to know?

BRIAN. I really believe that there was no one there for you.

MARC. What do you mean?

BRIAN. Nobody talked you through this?

MARC. Erin wouldn't even talk to me anymore ...

ERIN. That's not really true ...

BRIAN. No. I —

MARC. Oh, you mean like counselors?

BRIAN. Yeah. Or — what about your parents?

MARC. I don't talk to my dad and he doesn't talk to me and my real dad didn't even know. My mom was like, "figures ... "

BRIAN. So you are stupid.

MARC. Don't call me that. Don't say I'm stupid. Not you ...

BRIAN. Who better than me?

MARC. Because I can't hear that from you. *(Liz enters.)*

ERIN. Wouldn't you say that what you did was stupid?

MARC. I know it was stupid. I know it was stupid, alright? I feel

27

like I really have this gun on me and I'll never be able to get rid of it — like it's part of me now, okay? But —

LIZ. May I have that gun?

MARC. Why do you want it?

LIZ. I want you to give me that gun. *(Marc goes to Liz.)*

MARC. Here. Take it.

LIZ. This is you. *(She dry-fires into the trees.)* This is you. *(She fires up over Dragon's Tongue.)*

ERIN. I don't think that's necessary. You're as bad as he could have been.

LIZ. You don't?

ERIN. No.

LIZ. You don't really know anything about it, though, do you?

ERIN. I know enough.

LIZ. You may never know enough about it.

ERIN. Not the way you do. But —

BRIAN. I can't do this anymore.

MARC. Please —

BRIAN. Liz, please ... *(Liz goes to Brian and takes his hand.)*

MARC. Please ...

ERIN. Let it go, Marc.

MARC. Talk to me, man, talk to me ... *(Liz and Brian are gone.)* TALK TO ME! *(Marc and Erin are alone. He looks at her, unable to communicate his pain.)*

ERIN. ... I ... *(Blackout. Loud music. The lights come up on Marc at his desk. He's writing in his notebook, listening to a Walkman. Miss K enters.)*

MISS K. Take those off. *(Pause.)* TAKE THOSE OFF! *(Marc looks up, removes the headset.)*

MARC. Sorry.

MISS K. I want you to take this home with you and read it a couple of times. We're going to do another make-up test Monday. I also want you to have that essay for me.

MARC. What essay?

MISS K. Solving your problem.

MARC. You told me I still had time for that.

MISS K. You don't have that much time left. How much more do you need?

MARC. I don't know.

MISS K. Wednesday then.

MARC. Well ... okay.

MISS K. Go on. Get out of here. It's Friday and I don't want to be here any more than you do.

MARC. I can go and I won't get in trouble?

MISS K. What would I tell them?

MARC. See you Monday. *(He starts out.)*

MISS K. Tell your mom I said hi. *(He leaves.)* I guess ... *(She sits a moment, looking out at the mountains.)*

MISS K. ... What is my history...? *(The sun sets and Miss K and the classroom are gone. As darkness falls we hear a soft breeze begin to blow. Brian and Liz return to their picnic. We hear only the breeze and birds fussing in the trees. Liz packs up the picnic as Brian picks up his camera. The breeze stops blowing and the birds stop singing. Liz kisses Brian good-bye.)*

LIZ. I wish you'd come with me. Come with me now and we'll call your mom. It's supposed to rain anyway.

BRIAN. No ... go ahead. I want to stay and get as much of this as I can. This light's too good. I'll walk back.

LIZ. Bye ... *(She backs off. Brian changes the lens on his camera and begins shooting. He takes several shots and the daylight fades. Several variations of light hit Dragon's Tongue as Brian photographs the rocks and the shadows the light casts. Suddenly from off: drunken yelling and whooping. Brian pays no attention to this. He aims his camera toward the top of Dragon's Tongue and shoots as a bag full of empty beer cans is thrown across the stage, spilling garbage all over the rock and below. Brian stops taking pictures and looks at the garbage in disbelief. He looks up as Chris runs onto the rock.)*

CHRIS. What the fuck are you lookin' at, fuckin' faggot? *(Jim enters from below, followed by Marc.)*

BRIAN. I'm ... *(Jim rushes to beat Brian to the backpack and camera cases.)*

JIM. You're wrecking our party, man.

BRIAN. I'm leaving. Alright? I'm leaving —

JIM. What's this?

BRIAN. What are you doing with — hey that's my ... *(Chris jumps off the rock and grabs the other case.)* Come on, guys. Don't

— give that back to —

CHRIS. ... Huh? Come on guys...? Give that back ... What're you doin' here anyway?

BRIAN. I was just taking a few — I was working. I'm leaving. I —

JIM. What's the matter?

CHRIS. *(Dumping the contents of a bag.)* What is all this shit?

BRIAN. What are you doing? Give me that —

CHRIS. *(Hurling one of the cases into the rocks.)* That? Let you have that?

MARC. Oh shit ... let him ... come on, Chris, man ... *(Brian tries to retrieve his belongings.)*

BRIAN. Do you have any idea how much this —

JIM. This is our place — who said you could be here? *(Chris shoves Brian across the bluff. Brian crashes into Marc.)*

BRIAN. Come on. I just want to leave. Okay? Just let me go. I don't want to —

CHRIS. No. I think you wrecked our party, man. What are you gonna do about that?

JIM. Yeah, man. I think you killed my buzz.

BRIAN. *(To Marc.)* Come on ... please ... man ...

JIM. Listen to this fuckin' —

BRIAN. — just let me — *(Instantly the lights begin to burn white-hot on Marc and Brian and grow dark on the others. Brian is no longer fearing for his life and looks Marc in the eyes. The lights get hotter and more intense as he speaks.)* Isn't this where you fucked up? Everything else was just a glitch, wasn't it? Huh? Oh ... yeah, a "glitch." For a minute I thought you were different. There was a second when I thought you were going to make them let me go, but you didn't. One second. Is that your history? Did you think about me? Did you? Were you so hammered that you just saw some *thing* that was in your way? What did you see in that second? What did you think? Did you hate yourself so much for what you thought you'd never be that you had to take it out on me? How long will it take you to figure out that one second? You could have helped me. You could have — you stupid, pathetic — *(The light of the sunset immediately bleeds into red and the white-hot light on Marc and Brian follows suit. Jim lets out with an animal yell. Brian is back in the moment.)* ... help me ...

MARC. ... you fucking coward. *(Marc shoves Brian viciously in the chest and he goes flying into the arms of Jim and Chris.)*

JIM. You know what they used to do to trespassers ...

CHRIS. *(Pulling Brian up by the collar.)* Hey. How much is that camera worth, anyway?

JIM. *(Pulling him away from Chris.)* Yeah. Maybe we'll just take it and sell it.

MARC. *(Pulling him away from Jim.)* You should have just bolted, man. You should have just ... *(Brian struggles to break free from Marc. He runs toward the rocks.)*

JIM. — GET HIM — *(Chris dives toward Brian and Jim rushes him. Marc stands alone as the others begin to beat the shit out of Brian. A moment and Marc runs off as the lights slam to black. Darkness. A moment, then in the dark, we hear:)*

MISS K. You know Marc isn't as bad as you thought he was. *(Pause.)*

ERIN. Marc who?

MISS K. "Marc who?" You know who I'm talking about. *(The lights slowly come up on Miss K and Erin, barely illuminating their faces. It's as if they were sitting at home watching television.)*

ERIN. ... yeah ...

MISS K. He admires you.

ERIN. Yeah. Well ...

MISS K. Well?

ERIN. What...?

MISS K. Whatever you may think of him ... he ... still likes and admires you. Doesn't that change anything for you?

ERIN. It might have, until he got in trouble — not anymore.

MISS K. What do you mean 'til he got in trouble? No one ever found a gun, Erin.

ERIN. Yet ... What's next, Mom? What does he have to do to make you see that he's no good? You know he still hangs out with those assholes — *(She pauses to correct her language.)* ... With Jim and Chris. Maybe there wasn't a gun and they were just gonna take that kid's money. But maybe there is a gun and he'd have done it, too, I just know it, and so do you. He used to be nice and everything, I guess. He was hard to get to know. It's kinda like two Marcs: Marc before he got hurt and Marc after he got hurt. Before he got hurt, he was okay, and you'd get close

31

enough and you'd deal with it 'cause we were all on teams, and he was kind of there, but after he got hurt … I don't know. I thought it was kind of weird, but … I mean, we all wear our team jackets, you know? Tony Miller still wears his even though he quit playing football, but. Marc always wore his jacket. He always wore it, like he was just a little more proud of it than anybody else. I noticed that after he came back to school … and he couldn't play anymore … he never wore his jacket again. And … it's like, since then, I don't know. I still … I don't want to have anything to do with him and I think they should have just kicked him out. What's he going to need a diploma for anyway? He's not going to use it.

MISS K. I swear we're not talking about the same young man.

ERIN. Hello! Who are you? Do you really think he's not on best behavior in front of you? Come on, Mom. Marc the suspected arms dealer … He probably calls you "ma'am," too.

MISS K. Just so he can come back to school. Do you think that badly of me? Do you think I can't spot some hopeless case, after all this time? Erin?

ERIN. … God, Mom. I just think …

MISS K. I think you're being too hard. I think you've lost your judgment.

ERIN. Well. I told him he should·'t be hanging out with Jim and Chris. I knew they'd talk him into doing something stupid. What'll they talk him into next? Huh? *(The two of them stare ahead. What little light there is on them slowly begins to fade out and begins to fade up on Dragon's Tongue. Miss K and Erin sit in silence. We see Brian's body in the ghostly light on the rocks. He is lying on his back, torso toward the tip of the Tongue. His arm, shoulder and head are hanging off the side. Liz walks on and looks up at Brian. Marc walks on and looks at Liz, then up at Brian.)*

LIZ. Sleepwalking in a bad dream?

MARC. Yes.

LIZ. … sleepwalking in a nightmare. For the …

MARC. … rest of my life. *(Marc climbs up the rocks and bends down to Brian.)*

LIZ. I let him stay.

MARC. I left. *(Marc runs his hands through Brian's hair and across his bloody face and chest. When his hands are covered with blood, Marc stands up again.)*

LIZ. It was supposed to rain. *(Marc wipes the bright red blood across his white T-shirt. The lights burn bright on him. The color of the blood is brilliant. He looks down at Brian, then at Liz. Marc lowers and extends his arms to display his bloody palms.)*

MARC. … I left … *(He looks down at his bloody hands. A moment … he smears Brian's blood across his face. The lights no longer burn so hot on Marc … and slowly fade to black.)*

ACT TWO

The lights come up on the bluff. Brian's body is in the same position. Marc is gathering Brian's belongings. He kneels down and picks up one of the cameras, inspects it and puts it in a case. Brian lifts his arm and head. Marc moves to the backpack and stops when he sees Brian struggle to sit up.

MARC. I ... I got your stuff gathered up. For you. I think it's all ...

BRIAN. Why are you here?

MARC. I tried to help.

BRIAN. Who are you trying to help?

MARC. I just need to —

BRIAN. You need to get out of here. You need to let me go —

MARC. I can't. I don't think I'll ever be able to ...

BRIAN. That's your problem. *(He's climbed down from the rock and goes to Marc.)*

MARC. I know that. What do you think I'm trying to do?

BRIAN. Live my life.

MARC. No.

BRIAN. Really?

MARC. I'm trying to ...

BRIAN. *(Taking the cases from Marc.)* Let me go. *(Brian walks away. Marc watches him leave. He walks right past Liz, who enters with a bunch of flowers. She walks to the foot of Dragon's Tongue and places the flowers there. She bursts into tears. Marc does not move. A moment, then she turns away from the rocks and sees Marc.)*

LIZ. *(Moving to Marc.)* One of these days. *(She sucks back her tears, walks toward him but stops.)* ... you're going to hear from me. *(She walks out. Marc stands in stunned silence. The lights grow softer, it gets cooler, and Marc enters the classroom. He sits at his desk and holds a small package. Miss K enters.)*

MISS K. You're early again. Did you miss me?

34

MARC. I guess. I didn't think about it.

MISS K. Oh, you flatterer, you.

MARC. So, like ...

MISS K. What are you going to do with yourself after today?

MARC. What do you mean?

MISS K. Now that we're finished ...

MARC. Yeah. That. I know. I don't know.

MISS K. You know I'm going to recommend that you be allowed back in school. I've already discussed it with Mr. Lange. You passed with flying colors.

MARC. Yeah?

MISS K. You knew you were going to pass.

MARC. I figured, I mean ...

MISS K. There is one little thing.

MARC. What?

MISS K. You never did give me the first thing I asked for.

MARC. What?

MISS K. What ... what ...

MARC. ... come on. What? Didn't I give you?

MISS K. Your history. Your problem.

MARC. I ... just didn't finish it yet. I'll give it to you. I swear ... *(Pause.)*

MISS K. I ran into your mom at the Quick Stop.

MARC. Do you like meet everybody at the Quick Stop?

MISS K. She's not the way I remembered her ... All this time, and it never occurred to me that she was your mother ... All this time.

MARC. What do you mean?

MISS K. One can see someone and ... sometimes the connection just isn't there, I guess. One can look at another person and see them or choose not to see them. I had to have seen your mother before — remembered her. But until ... She thanked me ...

MARC. Yeah? *(Pause.)*

MISS K. So what are you going to do with yourself now that you're going to graduate?

MARC. I don't know.

MISS K. I think now is a really good time to think about it — you've only got three months.

MARC. I guess. I mean. What...?

MISS K. You have ... Have you applied to any colleges at all, Marc?

MARC. Not really.

MISS K. Why not?

MARC. Because ... I thought ... I mean there was ...

MISS K. *(Removing several brochures and applications from her case.)* Here. *(He tries to conceal the small package.)*

MARC. What's all this?

MISS K. These are for you.

MARC. Why?

MISS K. Because I want you to get away from here. I want you to go to school.

MARC. I — do you think I...?

MISS K. Yes, Marc. There were no guarantees you were ever going to get a football scholarship even if you hadn't gotten hurt in that accident and you still played. I think it's wrong to let you think that you might have. I think it's worse to let you continue thinking that's all you had going for you. I think it's a shame you weren't pushed harder to do better, and it makes me very angry that you were allowed to slip the way you did. You didn't give me your history, but you proved to me that you deserve to come back to school. You worked hard enough to pass, so all I want you to do for me is fill these out. So you don't get a scholarship. Apply for every grant you can. You'll get them.

MARC. This is ... this is ...

MISS K. There isn't an application there for any of the local schools. They're all around the state, because I want you to go away to go to school. Get away from here, Marc. *(Silence.)*

MARC. Thanks ... I ... *(He takes the envelopes and goes back to his desk. Jim leaps on from the trees and whistles loudly through his fingers and teeth at Marc, who freezes with his back to both Miss K and Jim. He holds the package.)*

JIM. Hey, kid. *(Silence.)* You still gonna try and ignore me? Come on, Marco, man.

MARC. No.

JIM. *(He sits on a rock and lights up.)* Yeah, well. Whatever, I guess, huh? You did it. You made up for your dirty deed. Get to go back to school like all the other kids, and graduate and ... then what? After you give the cap and gown back what are you gonna wear?

For a minute, I guess, when everybody's all dressed the same and everybody's all equal, it'll be nice, right? Nobody'll notice the big fallen jock/hero. Nobody'll notice that you've got "failure" written on your forehead. For a second. But then you'll be you again and they'll all be just lookin' at you and whisperin' about you again. Who will you be? What happened to us? Why can't we be like we used to be? Huh? What happened, kid?

MARC. Because you're — you don't — you're just wrong ...

JIM. No, you're wrong. You cut yourself shaving — you bleed *me* ... I'll just kick back and wait. That's all.

MISS K. Go on, get out of here, but you stay in touch. If you need any help, you come to me. We ...

MARC. I got this for you. (*He all but jumps back at her and gives her the gift.*) I got that for you because ...

MISS K. Marc.

MARC. You said once that Erin made fun of you for liking them, so I got you one.

MISS K. Marc ... (*She opens the package and removes a figurine of a ceramic clown.*)

MARC. I never knew anybody who collected clowns.

MISS K. I told you Erin made fun of my clowns?

MARC. Yeah.

MISS K. Marc ... thank you ...

MARC. It's just ... it's nothin' ... really. It's just ... I didn't even get embarrassed buying it. (*He starts to go.*)

MISS K. No ... It ... it means a lot. (*He does not turn to look at her:*)

MARC. Miss K. That first day ... when you told me you wanted to hear what I had to say ... was the first time I ever ... that was the first time anybody ever made me feel like I had something to say except when I play football — used to. I guess ... if I ever had ... a ... I mean I never had a favorite teacher or anything, and I didn't figure I would 'cause ... you know ... I ... but. You're my favorite teacher I ever had, Miss K.

MISS K. ... That means more to me than you know, Marc ... it really ... does ... (*She leaves Marc and Jim alone. The lights slowly grow darker.*)

JIM. You know, I was jealous of you. Yeah. I don't think I ever let it show, but I was. Fuckin' — you — man. You know what really gets me? You go off and be Mr. Football and leave me sittin' with shit-for-brains Chris, and you really don't even change. I couldn't hate you even though I was jealous 'cause you didn't change. You treated us the same as you always did. Mystery Marc. You know what's funny? If I was you, I wouldn't have done what you did. I wouldn't 'a stood around — I'd 'a been fuckin' outta here, kid. Gone. That's part of the reason. I just wait. Look at me. Look at me you fuckin' — (*Marc doesn't turn. Jim busts down to Marc and grabs his face and forces their eyes to meet.*) I just wait because I know you better than you know yourself. I know you'll be back. You are such a natural-born fuck-up, kid, shit. You do your little make-up lesson and you pass and then you're right back where you started and guess what? In three weeks we're going to the bluffs and somebody's gonna die ... (*The lights go black. Crickets begin chirping. Stars begin to appear in the sky over the mountains. As the lights come up it is the middle of the night. Chris enters.*)

CHRIS. (*Trying to whisper.*) Marc. MARC. (*When we see him, he is a mess. He's in a cold, panic-stricken sweat.*) MARC!

MARC. (*Entering.*) Shut up, man. My mom's home tonight ... just ... don't wake her up.

CHRIS. Where the fuck did you go?

MARC. You're fuckin' crazy if you think I was gonna hang around there and help you beat the shit outta that guy.

CHRIS. You were just as —

MARC. Bullshit! I fucked with him a little, but when he was begging me and I pushed him, I realized that it was —

CHRIS. Shut up! Shut up, man, you were —

MARC. I pushed him. That's all I did.

CHRIS. Where'd you go, man? Where'd you go? Huh?

MARC. I ran. Okay? I ran outta the bluffs and ... what'd you do to him...?

CHRIS. What'd...? Huh? ... Marco, man ... I think we killed that guy ... (*Marc looks at him and starts to walk away, but stops.*)

MARC. What did you do?

CHRIS. Bullshit! BULLSHIT! You were there too! You were there too!

MARC. I was not there! I was not there!

CHRIS. We killed that guy. I know we killed that guy. What're we gonna do?

MARC. Where's the gun, Chris? Did you use the gun? Oh, fuck! Did you?

CHRIS. No. We just … No.

MARC. Why did you come here?

CHRIS. Where else can I go? What else am I supposed to do?

MARC. You fucking … — I am not — I did not —

CHRIS. YOU WERE THERE!

MARC. Get the fuck outta here, Chris …

CHRIS. You gotta tell me what to do, Marc. You gotta — that guy is dead, man, I saw him — *(Marc backs away; Chris rushes to him. Marc shoves him away.)*

MARC. How do you know…? Maybe he just got knocked out or something …

CHRIS. He fell, man, after … I … Jim … Jim … I … Jim was like crazy all of a sudden, I mean. You know how sometimes he's like … crazy Jim … you know? But this was different. He was like … he was like … his eyes, Marc, man, his eyes were like rollin' up into the back of his head and he … Marc, man … he kicked him in the head, he … He kicked him in the head and the guy, man, the guy. He — it was like Jim got into some other world, or something, man. Oh, FUCK! The guy got up and he started climbing the rocks to get away, man, he was slipping and he kept climbing the rocks and he got on top of the Dragon's Tongue and he just stopped and fell over, and, oh, fuck, he fell over and … Jim was just laughin' at him and … that guy …

MARC. Where's Jim? *(Jim, in the trees, lights a cigarette in the darkness.)*

CHRIS. I don't know … I don't know … I can't find him.

MARC. Look harder. *(Chris moves toward him, but Marc indicates it's a mistake.)*

CHRIS. Marc, man …

MARC. … look harder … *(Marc leaves Chris alone in the dark.)*

CHRIS. Oh, fuck … Oh, fuck … Oh, fuck … *(Yelling toward Marc, who is gone.)* He was dead! I checked! I checked! *(The stars burn brighter for a moment. Dragon's Tongue begins to glow and we see Brian's body again. Jim moves out of the trees to watch Chris, who runs to the rocks. He begins to climb up, yelling at Jim:)* Oh, shit,

39

man, I think you killed him! I think you killed him ... *(He reaches Brian and finds that he's dead. Jim drops the cigarette, steps on it and slowly walks away. Chris scurries down the rocks.)*

CHRIS. Oh, fuck ... *(Again alone, Chris walks in circles, stops, mumbles, takes a pint out of his back pocket and drinks.)* ... what am I gonna do what am I gonna do what am I gonna do ... *(He bursts into a fit of tears and his legs give out on him.)* ... we killed him we killed him we killed him ... *(Still on his knees, he removes the gun from the waist of his pants.)* ... oh god oh god oh god ... MARC! *(The light of the night sky darkens and Chris puts the gun under his chin. The lights slam to black and the gunshot echoes then slowly fades into a song like "Insomnia" by Faithless. A moment and the song fades away. The lights slowly come up on Miss K. She is staring out at the mountains as Erin enters.)*

MISS K. You heard?

ERIN. Only rumors. A lot of rumors. Will we ever...?

MISS K. Yes. But I wanted to tell you before you heard too much from everybody else.

ERIN. I basically just kept hearing that Marc got arrested for beating somebody up.

MISS K. Don Lange called me into his office. I've been teaching how long now and I still get nervous when I get called to the principal's office.

ERIN. What happened, Mom?

MISS K. Did you hear anything about Chris Brown?

ERIN. No.

MISS K. Didn't you tell me Marc told you that Chris had the gun he was supposedly selling?

ERIN. Yeah.

MISS K. Chris Brown blew his brains out with that gun last night.

ERIN. What?

MISS K. Jim and Marc were arrested. Apparently they'd been drinking and who knows what else and ... I don't know what they were doing but they beat the living daylights out of some grad student up in the bluffs. They beat the shit out of him and left him there. When he was found he was in a coma and died five or six hours later.

ERIN. I told you Marc was —

MISS K. You shut your mouth, Erin. I will not stand here and let you mouth off to me with some half-thought-through judgment when you still don't know the whole — Marc was the one who called the police. Well, he didn't call the police, he went to the police and he told them what happened. Chris went to see Marc late last night because he was scared. Marc left them at the bluffs. Jim and Chris did most of ... what was done. Chris got scared and turned to Marc. Marc made him leave to find Jim and Chris just ... I'm trying to picture Marc walking into the police station at three in the morning to tell them ... what ... They found Jim out at the truck stop trying to steal a car. He was actually running away.

ERIN. This is ...

MISS K. I just wanted you to know what really happened before it gets all blown out of proportion and ...

ERIN. ... are you ...

MISS K. No. I'm not.

ERIN. Let's go home.

MISS K. I don't want to go home.

ERIN. Come on, Mom.

MISS K. I was trying to remember Marc playing football. I wish I could. Boycotting athletics because of all the other budget cuts — except for ...

ERIN. You watched me at my track meets ...

MISS K. It wouldn't look so good to boycott my own daughter. I wish I could remember. You saw Marc play. Don said nobody ever really talked about how good he was because they were all afraid that mentioning it would make it disappear.

ERIN. There were better players in the state —

MISS K. But Marc was ours. If somebody now and then would have told him ...

ERIN. People did tell him.

MISS K. Saying "great game" isn't exactly what I'd call encouragement.

ERIN. Are you going to be like all —

MISS K. I'm not going to be LIKE anything, Erin. I am. And yes, I am going to be this way for a while. This didn't have to happen.

ERIN. Nothing ever has to happen, Mom. Patrick didn't ever do anything that stupid. You always —

41

MISS K. Don't speak to me this way. Don't —

ERIN. I don't want to talk about this with you right now, okay?

MISS K. No. It's not okay. I think you and I will be having this conversation for as long as I'm your mother and you're my daughter, because I don't see you accepting me for who I am.

ERIN. What does that mean? Accepting you for who you are? You're my mother and you're a teacher and that's it. Just because you're a teacher doesn't mean you have to like carry the weight of the world on your shoulders. God, Mom, you feed all the stray dogs and cats in the neighborhood and our own pets roll their eyes. I've seen them do it. Your own dog and cat roll their eyes, so is it any wonder that, like I roll my eyes at you? Your students aren't your kids and they aren't stray pets. One of your Mind Matter Brainiacs gets a B in something and you mope for a week. What did you expect from Marc? Huh? You're supposed to take care of me. You're supposed to worry about me. They all have their own families to take care of them. I ... don't get it. I just don't get it.

MISS K. I know that. I know that. I agreed to take Marc on and that meant I'd give him everything I had to give. You know I'm an all or nothin' kinda gal, Erin. I always have been and you're not going to change me. I look at you and I see all the things I did right and I'm so proud of you. I'm so proud of you. And ... then I look at you and see that you can turn your emotions on and off just like ...

ERIN. ... like what?

MISS K. Sometimes I wish I could do it. I have to do what I do because I've always had to believe in something. Sometimes it's hard, and sometimes it hurts, but ...

ERIN. But ... couldn't you have ... didn't you see that it was too late for Marc ... Mom?

MISS K. No. It wasn't ... I knew he wasn't a whiz kid, but he deserved more than he got. We failed. We failed Marc.

ERIN. Marc failed himself.

MISS K. If he felt he had something, anything to hang onto I don't believe he'd have —

ERIN. No one twisted his arm to —

MISS K. No one twisted it to keep him away either. Do you remember the first time you met Patrick?

ERIN. ... no ...

MISS K. You accept Patrick as a part of our lives, don't you?

ERIN. Yeah.

MISS K. You speak the way you do about Marc, but Patrick is no different.

ERIN. Yes he —

MISS K. Patrick comes over to see us when he ... when he needs to ... when he knows to stay out of trouble. We accept him. He knows we do. You know he's still got a reputation around town. But that doesn't stop you from sitting on the front porch talking to him for three hours in front of God and everybody, does it?

ERIN. No.

MISS K. And you don't mind when he fixes the cars, do you?

ERIN. No ... But I grew up knowing him. It's almost like he's just an older brother or a cousin or something like that. It's not like it used to be ... even when I was a little kid, Mom. Even Pat knows that. I just don't want you to get hurt. Any kind of hurt. It scares me. I can't wait until I'm done with this school and ...

MISS K. ... I'm not going to get hurt ...

ERIN. ... and I wish you could leave it too after I graduate ... *(Erin walks out. Liz walks in. The lights change to denote a change in time.)*

LIZ. Excuse me.

MISS K. Yes? *(She suddenly recognizes Liz.)*

LIZ. I'm —

MISS K. I know. May I —

LIZ. I. I wanted to — I need to tell you how — sorry I am for ...

MISS K. How sorry you are? What are you sorry for, Liz? What could you be sorry for?

LIZ. You tried to speak to me ... several times ... at the court-house. I was ... I didn't — let you. I should have. I was ...

MISS K. No. You were —

LIZ. I was rude. It was rude ... to have ...

MISS K. It was a terrible time. It was a terrible thing to go through. I should never have imposed on you to begin with. Sometimes I — I get passionate and I let myself get carried away with an idea and ... that gets in the way of my better judgment. It was inappropriate to — would you like to sit?

LIZ. I get passionate too. Maybe that's why I — may I ask you something?

MISS K. Please.

LIZ. Why do you think I came to see you ... instead of — I'm here because of Marc McGettrick, you know?

MISS K. I know.

LIZ. I came to see you ... you instead of ... *(Liz bursts out laughing.)* I'm sorry. I'm sorry. I don't mean to laugh, I ... this is ridiculous. I don't know why I ... instead of his parents. *(The laughter stops.)*

MISS K. That's fine. It's understandable — I haven't seen them either. I haven't gone to — I supported Marc, as his teacher, it's under —

LIZ. I wanted to be a teacher.

MISS K. You wanted to be? Why aren't you?

LIZ. I wasn't strong enough. I'm *not* strong enough.

MISS K. I don't believe that.

LIZ. Yes you do. *(Pause.)*

MISS K. No. Then tell me why you aren't strong enough?

LIZ. I guess I'm not ... I'm a ... I'm a realist. Or maybe I'm just ... I don't have what it takes to fight it out.

MISS K. That sounds like bullshit to me, Liz.

LIZ. Well. I just wanted to apologize to you for ... *(She starts to go.)*

MISS K. Why didn't you go see Marc's parents. Or did you?

LIZ. I told you I'm not — no. I didn't. I drove past their house. I drove past that place, that roadhouse his mother runs ... I almost went in. I had this perverse ... feeling ... I wanted to go in there just to make her look at me and ... I'd never felt anything like it in my life. I almost got sick in the car.

MISS K. I'm glad you didn't go in.

LIZ. Two really drunk truckers walked out and I drove away.

MISS K. Probably former students of mine. I don't know what's worse — teaching in a big city where one might never see a student again, or teaching here where one sees all of them all of the time — even if I didn't realize it ...

LIZ. I should ... I ... I want to cry, again, but I have no more tears. I just ...

MISS K. You should be a teacher. It's not too late.

LIZ. Oh. It is ...

MISS K. It's never too late. We're all teachers, Liz. Some of us just get paid.

LIZ. And it's not enough. Is it, Miss K? *(Pause.)* I just wanted to say I was sorry for ... *(She starts out, and stops.)* I can't do this. I ... I got a letter from ... him. *(Pause.)*

MISS K. From Marc?

LIZ. I can't read it. Could you? *(Pause.)*

MISS K. Eventually. Probably. You can ... will ... *(Silence.)*

LIZ. ... thank you ... *(She walks out. Miss K sits a moment and then takes a manila envelope from under a file and opens it. She removes a black-and-white composition book.)*

MISS K. ... Marc, Marc, Marc ... *(She walks out. The lights fade to black. A moment and we hear the sound of prison doors opening and shutting. The lights come up on Marc, dressed in a prison uniform. He's alone sitting at a table waiting for a visitor. Liz enters.)*

LIZ. Did you ever think you'd see me?

MARC. No. I ... I don't know. I ...

LIZ. Why did you write me this letter?

MARC. ... because ...

LIZ. Oh, come on. I came all the way out here to see you, you can do better than that. *(Silence.)* Fine. I'll leave.

MARC. Did you read it?

LIZ. Eventually.

MARC. I wanted you to —

LIZ. I know ... I know you didn't ... I don't know what you want from me. I know what you want. But I ... *(She takes a folded-up letter from her pocket.)* I don't know why I came here. I — no. I do. I don't understand it but I ... I know you didn't kill him. I know you were the one who went to the police. I know you didn't kill him, but ... I think you ... killed me. You helped to kill ... I didn't read your letter for a long time. I kept looking at it and looking at it and ... I'd put it away. I put it in the bottom of a drawer and tried to forget about it. I'd walk into our house and Brian wouldn't be there ever again but you were there. Your letter was there. You were in my house and I hated you and I ... I hated you so much. I'd take my shoes off and I'd walk barefoot across this old carpet. I'd feel the soft, worn wool on the soles of my feet and I'd remember that that was the first thing Brian and

45

I bought together. We saved for three months to buy that old carpet and I'd feel it on the bottoms of my feet and I'd think of Brian and I'd remember that he was dead and that I'd never see him again. That he'd never be back. But you were in *our* house. You were there but Brian wasn't. But I couldn't throw your letter away. I couldn't read it, but I couldn't throw it away. If I hated you for what you did — I hated you more for ... sending yourself to me. I thought ... how dare you? What gives you the right to do that to me? Hadn't you done enough?

MARC. That's not what —

LIZ. No. Shut up. I don't want to hear anything you ... Everything I knew up to that point in time, I don't know anymore. Everything I believed in no longer exists. Everything I touch doesn't feel the same and it seems like all I have left is you. So ... I read it. *(She unfolds the paper but she doesn't look at it.)* I took it out of the drawer and I looked at it for days. I'd pick it up now and then and let it burn my hands. It felt like it was burning my hands. I sat down at our table and I opened it and ... I was struck by your handwriting. I looked at the words you'd written, but I wasn't reading them. I was looking at the nice handwriting and thinking that you ... how could somebody with such nice handwriting do what you did. Brian had horrible handwriting ... you don't. Brian is dead ... you aren't. *(Silence.)* So I read your words. I read your letter.

MARC. Please ...

LIZ. No. I don't ... I ... don't know what to do yet. I don't know what to feel. I don't hate that you got the reduced sentence, that you're going to be free in a couple of months. I'm not afraid of you. I'm glad the other one is ... He got what he deserved. He's a killer and he got what he deserved. I don't know anything about you. Marc. I don't want to know anything about you — other than what I already know ... what I heard at the trial. I want you to know what I've told you today. What you've done to me. I don't ... I want ... I don't care how you feel. And that makes me ... *(Silence.)* That makes me ... ache ... *(Silence.)* That you ... That I don't care ... *(Marc tries to wipe tears from his eyes but can't move.)*

MARC. I saw that story the newspaper did about him. I didn't know he was going to work there. That he —

LIZ. Say his name.

MARC. ... That Brian ... was a photographer. They printed all those pictures he took in the paper. ... the pictures he took that night. Of Dragon's Tongue. Before we got there. He was living his life and doing what he did and then we got there and ... and I saw those pictures and I ... can't stop thinking about those pictures ... and I'm so ... I'm so, so sorry that ... Brian ...

LIZ. One of these days things will change. I know that. One of these days things will be different. One of these days I'll remember what happened and I'll remember that it was supposed to have rained but it didn't — so we had a picnic ... and ...

MARC. If it rained like it was supposed to —

LIZ. — I wouldn't — Brian wouldn't be dead.

MARC. Please let me —

LIZ. No. I don't want you to have anything. I won't let you have anything.

MARC. I don't want anything.

LIZ. Oh really...?

MARC. I just ...

LIZ. What is this then?

MARC. I only ... I wrote you to ... I thought you ...

LIZ. Would understand.

MARC. No. I ... I know that isn't going to —

LIZ. Not going to happen.

MARC. ... no ...

LIZ. Let me ask you something...?

MARC. Yeah. Okay ...

LIZ. Wh ... *(She folds and unfolds the letter.)* ... No. I don't know now ... if I'll ever be able to forgive you. I hope I can, but I ... don't know that I'll ever be able to let you know. I do not ever want to hear from you again. *(Silence. She unfolds his letter and presses it to the table.)* That's ... That's why I came here. I want ... I don't ever want that ... *(She stands and walks away as the lights fade. Brian has entered and sits on Dragon's Tongue. He's no longer bloodied. Marc sits at the table a moment before joining Brian on the rocks.)*

BRIAN. Are you finished with me?

MARC. I think so.

BRIAN. Good. I hope you know that you can't ever make anything of me. I won't ever be anything you'll understand.

MARC. I think I can now. I just had to know ... you. I just had to ... I had to find out that ... I thought I could make you fit — in my mind. I thought I could get a handle on you and know you somehow and know what I did. Know what I let happen ... I mean ... and ... know what I helped to take. Away from you. For the rest of my life, I'm going to have you — here — and I just had to ... I don't know, man, it's gonna be ... but, I ... I think what I think of you — the way I think of you can ... help ... me ...

BRIAN. The way you think of me...? The way you — think of me? So you can misinterpret me? Don't you know that the way you think of anything is probably wrong? The way anybody really thinks of anybody else is ... But, hey, man, that's your prerogative, isn't it? The way you think of me ... I was wrong, in the last few minutes of my life, when I saw the three of you. I thought you were the dangerous one. I thought ... in assessing the situation, that Chris was nervous, shaky — probably incapable; that Jim was, I don't know, for some reason, I thought he'd rather watch ... I don't know why, and he's the one who killed me. But — I thought it would be you. The one that looked strongest. I thought you'd be the one to see red. I thought I'd seen you so many times before: in college bars, the one always getting into fights; at ball games looking for trouble; so many times, so many places. I swear to you. I thought you'd be the one to see red. I was wrong. The way you think of me. Forever, now, I'm going to wonder about the woman I love. Every day I'll miss that I could have learned more about her and learned how wrong I was about her in every way. I'll miss everything so much now, but mostly I'll miss being wrong about things and learning from that. My life, and Liz, and my plans. I had so many plans. I was going to show people that this place was so beautiful. Still. In the light, sometimes, you can't even see the graffiti — that's why I stayed. For the light. I was going to develop the film in this amazing hyper-color, you know? And the rocks would be so red that against the sky they'd look black and the trees would be so green they'd be blue and everything would look so perfect that you'd think God just created the place right then and there. You know people are wrong about this place, don't you? Because people really only see what they want to see. Believe what they want to believe. Most people. You'd think I'd be able to see you ... now, and know you. But I can't. Because I'm ... The way you think of me? That must be the way people think of this place ... *(For a moment, the lights take on a harsh quality and we see for the first time that the rocks are covered in graffiti. This is only for a second and then the lights are back, even softer than before, and again, we do not see graffiti.)* I always tried to convince people to think differently, or at least to look at things differently. Myself, too. To capture the truth. Maybe that's why I wanted to work for the newspaper. I couldn't take the pictures I wanted unless I took the pictures I had to take. I think I would have done a nice job of the pictures I took here that day ... but I don't know. If somebody else developed them they won't be what I meant, will they? How could they be? What you think of me...? What does that mean, anyway?

MARC. Everybody always pretends they don't care what other people think of them. But don't you think that's why so many people get in trouble? Because they do care? I care. I can say that now. I can't pretend I don't anymore, either. What I think of you? I don't know what hurts worse now ... caring or pretending I don't. I did look at you and ... I saw what I wanted to see. And I was wrong, wasn't I? *(Marc jumps off the rock and the lights fade to a dim glow on Brian.)*

BRIAN. Will you let me go now?

MARC. I hope so ... *(Brian walks away through the rocks and is gone in the darkness. In the darkness we hear the prison sounds again. When the lights come up, Miss K is sitting at the table with Marc.)*

MISS K. I've never been in prison before.

MARC. I can't believe you're here.

MISS K. I heard you were getting an early release, so I thought I'd just pop on up and see what prison was like. I don't expect to get this chance ever again and I didn't think I should miss it. *(He looks at her like she has two heads.)*

MARC. I missed you.

MISS K. Well, it's been a good long time.

MARC. Why did you come? I mean, I'm really happy but I —

MISS K. Because you finally sent me your history.

MARC. Did you read it?

MISS K. I certainly did.

MARC. I failed.

MISS K. I'd have given you a good solid B.

MARC. Never will get that A, will I?

MISS K. You would have but it was late, so ... This is so strange. Prison is so strange.

MARC. I'm not gonna miss it.

MISS K. I hope ... you don't mind that I came.

MARC. No. No. Please ... I ...

MISS K. Did you hear much ... from ... anybody...?

MARC. Not really. No.

MISS K. Marc ... did your mother or ...

MARC. Not really. No. A couple letters now and then from my little sister, but ... maybe just one from my mom. She only came once ... I got a letter from my real dad, though.

MISS K. Really?

MARC. It was nice to get it. He didn't have too much to say. I guess ...

MISS K. Erin said she sent you a —

MARC. Yeah. She sent me a card.

MISS K. I'm glad.

MARC. Yeah. That was nice ...

MISS K. Patrick Sisson got married.

MARC. Really...? You must be all jealous.

MISS K. No, I think his wife is all jealous. *(A moment and he gets the joke and they laugh.)*

MARC. I thought about you a lot. I really did.

MISS K. That's nice ... thank you.

MARC. I really did. It meant ... a lot to me that you ... that you came to the ... you know ... every day, and that you said those nice things about me to the papers.

MISS K. I just ... what happened — well. You gave me a lot of thinking to do, Marc. A lot of thinking to do, and I ... What made you do it? What made you go with them? You had so little time left before graduation and, you just got back on track ... I went to the trial because I wanted to know. That you walked away was good, but ... *(Pause.)*

MARC. I guess ... I could have ... If I stayed could I have stopped Jim? ... from doing that? I don't know. I just don't know ... I ...

50

MISS K. I guess it's a little late, but … are you alright?

MARC. Yeah, I'm … I don't feel like I've slept since I got here. I just … I just … it's like that part of my mind. I think I still have the last song I heard in my head. You know when that happens — you hear a song and it stays in your head and tortures you until you hear another song? It's like that's what happened to me. I remember leaving Chris and going back in our house and sitting on my bed and … My sister was playing this song … "Insomnia" or something and … I sat there listening to it wondering what I was gonna do. Just sitting there not knowing what to do. I got up and got dressed and walked out of the house. And that song was in my head. I walked down the street and that song was in my head. I kept walking and it was playing in my mind. I walked past the Quick Stop and it was playing in my head and I wished it had been raining and I wished that you had been at the Quick Stop … because I would have … you would have helped me … I think … but there was no one there and I bought cigarettes and the song was in my head. I walked into the police station and I just stood there and the song wouldn't leave my head. You know … *(He lights a cigarette.)* It was weird because it seems like I was standing there for a really long time, like, sweating and … I must have looked guilty of something … because I guess I was, but … it seemed like nobody noticed me. I went up to that cop at the desk and … In my mind … with the song … I was thinking, like, how do I tell this cop that I think I know that this guy is … dead. *(Silence.)* Nothing's been in my mind since. It seems like. But I know that's not true. A lot's been in my mind. … That guy's … Brian Penn's wife came to see me.

MISS K. … did she…?

MARC. I sent her a letter.

MISS K. Ahhhh …

MARC. I thought about it a while before I did it.

MISS K. Why did you —

MARC. — I didn't want her to think I didn't know what I … that I … I wanted her to know that I was so —

MISS K. — Have you heard anything about … Jim?

MARC. No. *(Pause.)* No. I … I … I hated him, and I wanted to kill him, but … it was because I blamed him, and I can't do that.

51

I can't blame him. Such a fucking — I'm sorry — I'm sorry. I …
MISS K. I know.
MARC. Chris … I still can't … I mean … what he did to him —
MISS K. There wasn't any indication that he was sui —
MARC. No. Chris was always — you know, nervous. I mean … I
— I walked away from that guy — Brian Penn. I walked away from
Chris. I left him … and told him to look for Jim. I … I didn't know
he'd … I forgot about the gun — he had that gun. I didn't know. I
swear to God I just … I mean what was I thinking? What was he
thinking? What were any of us thinking? You know? Miss K? If I
did have the gun and sold it … Chris would be alive, wouldn't he?
MISS K. Don't. Marc. Don't. If you'd sold that gun more people
might have … Don't. Chances are, Chris …
MARC. I mean … I get like, the worst headaches tryin' to just
figure that out and … there's nothin' there. I just don't have any
idea what … Sometimes … I … Did I let two people die? Miss K?
Did I do that? Is it … my fault … that two people died…?
MISS K. It is not your fault that Chris Brown killed himself.
Marc. Please …
MARC. I … well … I just … Hey … I know my … that note-
book must have been a mess. Thank you for reading it. It must
have been hard … me thinking — writing about what I thought.
Imagining Brian Penn … what he might say, who he was. And his
wife coming to see me … and Erin …
MISS K. Any time.
MARC. What can I … what am I gonna do when I …
MISS K. Well, you can't vote.
MARC. Yeah. That's probably gonna suck.
MISS K. Did you ever mail in those applications?
MARC. … you know … I thought about it and … I came here
instead …
MISS K. You've changed … you've certainly …
MARC. Yeah, but is that really good enough?
MISS K. It's necessary.
MARC. I mean … I guess there are a lot of things I could do …
but …
MISS K. … I imagine time goes slowly here …
MARC. Yeah. … yeah …

MISS K. I have a bit of time on my hands ...

MARC. What do you mean? A bit? It's summer, aren't you on —

MISS K. Oh, I'm on vacation, but I'm in school again. I'm getting my second Masters — in gifted and talented education ...

MARC. Yeah?

MISS K. Yeah. But I can ... I'll ... I'd like to help you ... if I can.

MARC. You ... haven't you done enough for me? I mean ... coming here even ...

MISS K. Maybe I feel the same about you that you felt about walking away from Brian Penn and leaving Chris alone ...

MARC. What do you mean?

MISS K. Erin said that nobody twisted your arm to make you go with Jim and Chris that night and —

MARC. — I guess that's true —

MISS K. — and I said that nobody twisted it to keep you from going.

MARC. I guess that's true too ... huh? Except me ...

MISS K. Why did you go, Marc?

MARC. Miss K ... I ... I still don't know why I went and I'll ... I ...

MISS K. Will you be going home? When you ...

MARC. I don't know. I really don't know ... *(Pause.)*

MISS K. I'm in prison ...

MARC. God, I wish I could leave with you ... now ... The closer I get to getting out the longer it seems to last ... *(Silence.)*

MISS K. I wish you could too ...

MARC. Yeah, man ... I can't wait ...

MISS K. What do you want to do first?

MARC. Well, just about anything'll be better than still being here ... *(He laughs, she joins him.)*

MISS K. ... Marc ...

MARC. God, I don't know ... there are so many things. So many things. To take a shower and ... for a long, long time, but it wouldn't wash it all away ... and like ...

MISS K. May I take you to dinner. Would you like that?

MARC. Really?

MISS K. Yeah. I'll take you to my favorite new restaurant. It's sooo good.

MARC. Why are you ... what ... I ... what did you mean when you said that maybe you felt like I did...?

MISS K. Maybe I just feel like I should have twisted your arm ... Or, maybe I just like guys who get in trouble. ... What else would you like to do? *(Pause.)* Marc?

MARC. Huh? I'm sorry ... I was just ...

MISS K. What else? What do you really want to do when ... *(Silence.)*

MARC. I'd ... *(He looks away for a moment and then looks back at her.)* ... really love for it to rain for a really, really long time, and ... I just want to sleep. I just want to sleep ... *(The lights slowly fade on them and:)*

Curtain

NEW PLAYS

★ **A LESSON BEFORE DYING by Romulus Linney, based on the novel by Ernest J. Gaines.** An innocent young man is condemned to death in backwoods Louisiana and must learn to die with dignity. "The story's wrenching power lies not in its outrage but in the almost inexplicable grace the characters must muster as their only resistance to being treated like lesser beings." —*The New Yorker.* "Irresistable momentum and a cathartic explosion…a powerful inevitability." —*NY Times.* [5M, 2W] ISBN: 0-8222-1785-6

★ **BOOM TOWN by Jeff Daniels.** A searing drama mixing small-town love, politics and the consequences of betrayal. "…a brutally honest, contemporary foray into classic themes, exploring what moves people to lie, cheat, love and dream. By BOOM TOWN's climactic end there are no secrets, only bare truth." —*Oakland Press.* "…some of the most electrifying writing Daniels has ever done…" —*Ann Arbor News.* [2M, 1W] ISBN: 0-8222-1760-0

★ **INCORRUPTIBLE by Michael Hollinger.** When a motley order of medieval monks learns their patron saint no longer works miracles, a larcenous, one-eyed minstrel shows them an outrageous new way to pay old debts. "A lightning-fast farce, rich in both verbal and physical humor." —*American Theatre.* "Everything fits snugly in this funny, endearing black comedy…an artful blend of the mock-formal and the anachronistically breezy…A piece of remarkably dexterous craftsmanship." —*Philadelphia Inquirer.* "A farcical romp, scintillating and irreverent." —*Philadelphia Weekly.* [5M, 3W] ISBN: 0-8222-1787-2

★ **CELLINI by John Patrick Shanley.** Chronicles the life of the original "Renaissance Man," Benvenuto Cellini, the sixteenth-century Italian sculptor and man-about-town. Adapted from the autobiography of Benvenuto Cellini, translated by J. Addington Symonds. "[Shanley] has created a convincing Cellini, not neglecting his dark side, and a trim, vigorous, fast-moving show." —*BackStage.* "Very entertaining…With brave purpose, the narrative undermines chronology before untangling it…touching and funny…" —*NY Times.* [7M, 2W (doubling)] ISBN: 0-8222-1808-9

★ **PRAYING FOR RAIN by Robert Vaughan.** Examines a burst of fatal violence and its aftermath in a suburban high school. "Thought provoking and compelling." —*Denver Post.* "Vaughan's powerful drama offers hope and possibilities." —*Theatre.com.* "[The play] doesn't put forth compact, tidy answers to the problem of youth violence. What it does offer is a compelling exploration of the forces that influence an individual's choices, and of the proverbial lifelines—be they familial, communal, religious or political—that tragically slacken when society gives in to apathy, fear and self-doubt…" —*Westword.* "…a symphony of anger…" —*Gazette Telegraph.* [4M, 3W] ISBN: 0-8222-1807-0

★ **GOD'S MAN IN TEXAS by David Rambo.** When a young pastor takes over one of the most prestigious Baptist churches from a rip-roaring old preacher-entrepreneur, all hell breaks loose. "…the pick of the litter of all the works at the Humana Festival…" —*Providence Journal.* "…a wealth of both drama and comedy in the struggle for power…" —*LA Times.* "…the first act is so funny…deepens in the second act into a sobering portrait of fear, hope and self-delusion…" —*Columbus Dispatch.* [3M] ISBN: 0-8222-1801-1

★ **JESUS HOPPED THE 'A' TRAIN by Stephen Adly Guirgis.** A probing, intense portrait of lives behind bars at Rikers Island. "…fire-breathing…whenever it appears that JESUS is settling into familiar territory, it slides right beneath expectations into another, fresher direction. It has the courage of its intellectual restlessness…[JESUS HOPPED THE 'A' TRAIN] has been written in flame." —*NY Times.* [4M, 1W] ISBN: 0-8222-1799-6

DRAMATISTS PLAY SERVICE, INC.
440 Park Avenue South, New York, NY 10016 212-683-8960 Fax 212-213-1539
postmaster@dramatists.com www.dramatists.com

NEW PLAYS

★ **THE CIDER HOUSE RULES, PARTS 1 & 2 by Peter Parnell, adapted from the novel by John Irving.** Spanning eight decades of American life, this adaptation from the Irving novel tells the story of Dr. Wilbur Larch, founder of the St. Cloud's, Maine orphanage and hospital, and of the complex father-son relationship he develops with the young orphan Homer Wells. "…luxurious digressions, confident pacing…an enterprise of scope and vigor…" –*NY Times.* "…The fact that I can't wait to see Part 2 only begins to suggest just how good it is…" –*NY Daily News.* "…engrossing…an odyssey that has only one major shortcoming: It comes to an end." –*Seattle Times.* "…outstanding…captures the humor, the humility…of Irving's 588-page novel…" –*Seattle Post-Intelligencer.* [9M, 10W, doubling, flexible casting] PART 1 ISBN: 0-8222-1725-2 PART 2 ISBN: 0-8222-1726-0

★ **TEN UNKNOWNS by Jon Robin Baitz.** An iconoclastic American painter in his seventies has his life turned upside down by an art dealer and his ex-boyfriend. "…breadth and complexity…a sweet and delicate harmony rises from the four cast members…Mr. Baitz is without peer among his contemporaries in creating dialogue that spontaneously conveys a character's social context and moral limitations…" –*NY Times.* "…darkly funny, brilliantly desperate comedy…TEN UNKNOWNS vibrates with vital voices." –*NY Post.* [3M, 1W] ISBN: 0-8222-1826-7

★ **BOOK OF DAYS by Lanford Wilson.** A small-town actress playing St. Joan struggles to expose a murder. "…[Wilson's] best work since *Fifth of July*…An intriguing, prismatic and thoroughly engrossing depiction of contemporary small-town life with a murder mystery at its core…a splendid evening of theater…" –*Variety.* "…fascinating…a densely populated, unpredictable little world." –*St. Louis Post-Dispatch.* [6M, 5W] ISBN: 0-8222-1767-8

★ **THE SYRINGA TREE by Pamela Gien.** Winner of the 2001 Obie Award. A breathtakingly beautiful tale of growing up white in apartheid South Africa. "Instantly engaging, exotic, complex, deeply shocking…a thoroughly persuasive transport to a time and a place…stun[s] with the power of a gut punch…" –*NY Times.* "Astonishing…affecting …[with] a dramatic and heartbreaking conclusion…A deceptive sweet simplicity haunts THE SYRINGA TREE…" –*A.P.* [1W (or flexible cast)] ISBN: 0-8222-1792-9

★ **COYOTE ON A FENCE by Bruce Graham.** An emotionally riveting look at capital punishment. "The language is as precise as it is profane, provoking both troubling thought and the occasional cheerful laugh…will change you a little before it lets go of you." –*Cincinnati CityBeat.* "…excellent theater in every way…" –*Philadelphia City Paper.* [3M, 1W] ISBN: 0-8222-1738-4

★ **THE PLAY ABOUT THE BABY by Edward Albee.** Concerns a young couple who have just had a baby and the strange turn of events that transpire when they are visited by an older man and woman. "An invaluable self-portrait of sorts from one of the few genuinely great living American dramatists…rockets into that special corner of theater heaven where words shoot off like fireworks into dazzling patterns and hues." –*NY Times.* "An exhilarating, wicked…emotional terrorism." –*NY Newsday.* [2M, 2W] ISBN: 0-8222-1814-3

★ **FORCE CONTINUUM by Kia Corthron.** Tensions among black and white police officers and the neighborhoods they serve form the backdrop of this discomfiting look at life in the inner city. "The creator of this intense…new play is a singular voice among American playwrights…exceptionally eloquent…" –*NY Times.* "…a rich subject and a wise attitude." –*NY Post.* [6M, 2W, 1 boy] ISBN: 0-8222-1817-8

DRAMATISTS PLAY SERVICE, INC.
440 Park Avenue South, New York, NY 10016 212-683-8960 Fax 212-213-1539
postmaster@dramatists.com   www.dramatists.com